# Frost

Written by Nancy O'Connor

**Flying Start**
to Literacy®

# Contents

# Introduction

Have you ever seen tiny ice crystals on the ground in the morning after a very cold, still night?

These ice crystals look like a light dusting of snow on the grass. When you walk on them, the ice crystals may crunch under your shoes. These ice crystals are frost.

Frost can also cover plants and trees. For fruit and vegetable farmers, frost can be deadly. Frost can kill their plants and destroy their crops. Farmers have to protect their crops from frost.

# Chapter 1

# What is frost?

Frost is frozen water. Water freezes at zero degrees Celsius.

Frost happens on cold nights when there are no clouds or wind. The air can become very cold and the temperature can drop to zero degrees Celsius. When this happens, ice crystals form.

Frost can form on plants and windows.

When the sun comes up, it melts the frost. The frost disappears.

7

# Killer frost

Frost can form on trees, fruits, vegetables and flowers.

For some plants, frost is dangerous. It can damage some fruits, vegetables and flowers, and it can kill some plants.

When frost covers a plant, ice crystals can form inside the plant. These ice crystals can make the cells inside the plant burst. This damages the plant, and sometimes kills it.

# Orange farms

Oranges are one of the many fruits that frost can damage. Farmers have to protect the oranges on the trees from frost.

Most orange trees flower in spring. The flowers become tiny fruit by the beginning of summer.

The fruit starts to ripen in autumn. The longer the oranges stay on the tree, the sweeter they become.

When winter arrives, the oranges are sweetening up and are ready to be picked. This is when frost can happen.

# Frosty oranges

When an orange is covered in frost, it gets very cold and freezes. Ice crystals form inside the orange's cells.

When the frost melts, the skin of the orange can get brown spots and the fruit can rot. The oranges may fall off the tree and will no longer be juicy or good to eat.

Farmers can lose a lot of money if the oranges on their trees are covered in frost. On very cold nights, farmers work hard to stop frost forming on the oranges.

## Chapter 3

# Fighting frost

Farmers fight frost using wind, smoke and water.

## Using wind

### Windmills

Some farmers use windmills to move the air around their crops. This stops frost from forming on the crops on still, cold nights.

The windmill pushes away cold air. It pulls in warm air from above the trees and blows it back down to the trees. This keeps the air around the trees warm so that frost cannot form.

14

# Helicopters

Some farmers use helicopters to stop frost.

The pilots fly close to the ground at night.
The blades on the helicopter mix the warm air
from above the trees with the cold air close
to the ground.  This keeps the air around
the trees warm so that frost cannot form.

Pilots may have to fly back and forth over the same trees every hour to keep the air temperature above freezing.

This is dangerous work because pilots have to fly in the dark and close to the ground.

# Using smoke

About a hundred years ago, a heater was invented that could be used to keep plants warm. This heater uses oil and is called a smudge pot.

The heaters are placed between rows of orange trees. Each heater has a round pot and a tall chimney.

On cold nights, farm workers put thick black oil into the smudge pots and then light them. The burning oil makes clouds of heavy black smoke which acts like a blanket for the trees.

The air around the trees stays warm so frost cannot form.

# Using water

Strange as it may sound, some farmers fight frost by freezing their oranges!

They use tall sprinklers to wet the orange trees.  When the temperature drops to zero degrees Celsius, the water on the oranges quickly turns into ice.

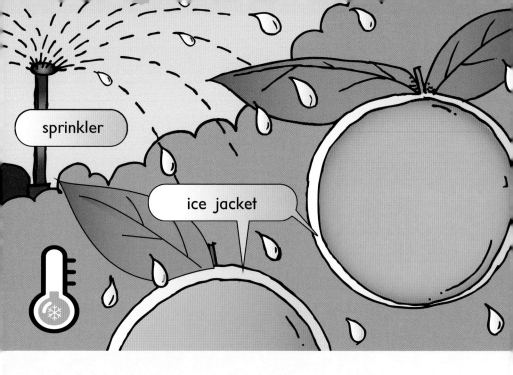

The ice around the big, thick-skinned orange protects it. The temperature inside the orange might get cold, but not so cold that ice crystals form.

With its "ice jacket", the orange will survive the cold night.

# Conclusion

Farmers have to watch the weather so they know when frosts are likely to happen. This helps them to protect their fruit and vegetables from killer frosts.

The next time you eat a juicy orange or drink a glass of orange juice, remember the frost-fighting farmers who helped that fruit survive!

# Glossary

**cells**  A cell is the smallest part of all living things. Every living thing is made up of millions of cells.

**chimney**  A tube through which smoke can rise and escape.

**ice**  Ice is frozen water.  It is water in a solid state.

**ice crystals**  Ice crystals form when water freezes and changes from a liquid into a solid.  When the crystals form, they make patterns.

**temperature**  The measurement that tells you how hot or cold something is, such as air or water.

**zero degrees Celsius**  This is the temperature at which water starts to freeze.